# NOTES FROM THE VOID

by

Ollie Shane

Copyright © 2025 Ollie Shane
Edited by Brittany McMunn
Cover design by Abigail Wild
Layout by Abigail Wild

978-1-958531-99-0 (paperback)
978-1-964885-00-1 (Epub)


All rights reserved. No part of this publication may be reproduced, distributed, or transmitted in any form or by any means, including photocopying, recording, or other electronic or mechanical methods, without the prior written permission of the publisher, except in the case of brief quotations embodied in critical reviews and certain other noncommercial uses permitted by copyright law.

For Mom, Dad and Pop

*also Lottie,*

*though I'm sure you would eat this*

# INTRODUCTION

If you're reading this, you have heard of me. Perhaps you are my friend, a member of my family, or just picked it up from the bookstore.

In the course of this collection, I hope you understand me as a poet and, or maybe even worthy of the title of "author."

Enjoy the ride. Don't think too much about literary devices you remember in the vague recesses of your memory from high school English.

# PART ONE:

# IMPATIENT IN INPATIENT

# PORTRAIT OF AN AUTHOR BEFORE A BREAKDOWN

Reader observe
me with my friend

we've been through some shit, who hasn't
in this, the end of history

a beloved
dystopia

they smile,
their mask covers it; a veil

I smile
But something's off

In my gaze
Something's wrong

Something lurks behind the camera
Pointed perpendicular, a propinquity to paradise

Your gaze is drawn
To the wound on my hand

I'd picked at it
Wanting to feel something

Something other
Then this Internet-laden void

Then this numbness creeps in
Fogging up my mind's glasses

I am a king


I can do
Anything.

# STIGMATA

my personal Jesus

Hanging by a precarious nail on a white wall marked
With the passage of numerous grandkids' frolics

Now one, left to care for herself
And the woman left to be
Her caregiver
She's
always lost in dreams

she thought she could be Jesus and I too
Felt the transference

One day, when she
Slept off the heat of noon
In her stifling bed,

I saw Jesus's wounds and thought
If you are human,
Can make eyes, and
Bleed like a sinner's transgressions in church

so can i

I can do it,
I said

And I opened my face
To reveal
A thousand eyes, scabbed
To see the world through your eyes
My personal Jesus.

# FRONT END CASHIER BLUES

can you work mornings

ur supervisor, stout
Covered in tattoos

Said

You, dumb
Said yes

So, here you are
19, young, full of

Libidinous thoughts

From 7 to 11 am
Monitoring seven machines

A hawk
For stealing

And other avarice
that we are

Prone to
Your supervisor

OLLIE SHANE

Clean kept as a tobacco addict
Curses at computers

Your coworkers
Have a tendency to wander

You're reminded of people who wander
Suffering from memory issues

You call his name
A nurse among the elderly

Is what you become
Clad in red rather than the blue scrubs

Of the nurses, you'll later see
After all this

After you've gone into another world
Where your family keep you

From making your hand a stab wound
Your father

Turned in your uniform and your supervisor
A kind woman

Said,
"She was the best worker I've ever had."

# THE 54321 GROUNDING TECHNIQUE AS A POEM

**5 things you can see:**
- The clear mucus of my tears, blinding me to the wonders of my room
- A mask with tears in it overlaps a painting of a girl reading a book
- Books stacked like kids' flimsy towers
- The huge tear in the fabric of the world
- A pale horse, ridden by a grinning skeleton

**4 things you can feel:**
- The shame of another breakdown here we fucking go, I think, just like it's been the last five years since your world turned upside down, since you first saw [ ] horizontal lines of horror from [ ] and even though you didn't whet the knife, it consumed you, it fucked you up so bad you still think of those cuts even when nothing triggers you, just to remember that summer day and the horror on her face, to remember the hell you've been through and the descent to its hottest place, to do nothing amid the swirl of frequent fights but to turn on the fan as if it will whirl away the hatred and the suffering you've dealt with and remembering the falsehood that it's [ ]'s fault
- The distant weight of my pillow beckoning me to sleep, "sleep please so you aren't half dead in zero period don't need to nap when you get home so you can do homework, sleep so you can understand math, sleep so you don't fall under" I ignore it

- Am I a spicy girl or something else; did puberty transform me into another strange monster, distant to everyone except her?
- The weight of sleep deprivation caused by the chaos of COVID

**3 things you can hear**
- Footsteps, fate's doomsday clock
- My brain scrambling for the coping mechanisms my parents pay $$$$ for; it can only find the command to cry
- The sound of the shower, manufactured rain making [ ] happier

**2 things you can smell:**
- Fear
- Blood

**One good thing you can name about yourself**
- The capability to endure (engraved in my bones from my tattooed heritage), even when language and fists and knives and guns and airplanes and raids succeed.

# PART TWO:

# I WANT DESIRE

# LOST BOI

I knew the words for my own desire
They ringed my mouth with black and red
For years I looked for a match like mine

I looked ardently for the same hues
I only saw blue and
Damn near drowned in their ocean
Then I found you
An angel in band tees and converse

I just thought my desire
To laugh at every joke
Was because you had humor
I mistook my red for just affection
"Just friends," I said

I look at the poems I wrote about you and I laugh

And now you gather wildflowers
You teach children about the joys of music

Some days, I watch you sidestep
Uninformed queries from well-meaning suburban mothers

On those days, I wake up
Wishing I knew how to bring out the pink from your lips.

OLLIE SHANE

# AFTER YOU'VE GONE

left me all alone
to drown in others' glares

left me to cry
on company time

left me for your beloved

continued
school in paradise

after you
destroyed any hint
of kissing you in the rain while other,
more sensible people ducked for cover

after you left me to defend what we did
reminded anyone with the slightest inkling of something
    more

that I loved you
like a friend loves another


bullshit
I loved you like a woman loves another

oh yes
I'm watching that lesbian romance shit
ya know, the slow burns that end in tender kisses, ardent caresses


yet you


ignorant

of my affections!

# WHAT IS A GIRL IF NOT AN OPEN WOUND?

*title after instagram artist girl of swords @grlofswords. She also has a bonfire store under girlofswords if you are so moved to buy some of her shirts.*

what is a girl if not an open wound
A series of sores
Viewed in flesh
Lumps where their presence
Is felt best

what is a girl if not a woman from Venus
beam'd down
To grace us with an ephemeral existence
Before—always a before—
Her life circuits out

who are you if not Plato's second half
Two souls,
Thunderously in love
only sever'd
By Zeus's lightning dick

who are you if not a yowling cat
Demanding my presence then yelling
When my hand touches some wound
Too close
To your furr'd belly

who am I if not a nurse on call?
 rousing from sleep
Seductive silence
 to deliver miracles
to demanding patients

who am I if not
an ordinary angel in extraordinary times?
I stare at the screen
Filled to the brim with important boredom
And wonder how I can transcend
My open wound: an eye
On the fucked up-ness of my mind.

# SOMEDAY I'LL BE OLLIE SHANE

*After ocean vuong*

It's been one year, not
A thousand
Calm down
Ok?


Don't fear the void, Ollie
Your body—strained as it is
Can change
Curves can be
Something in between

Doctors can help
To fit
The in-between
Of your gender

Your father's joy does not have to be
Imbued w/your name
He will love you regardless,
He said it himself,


You can check ur texts more often

-but i… my family—

No buts, Ollie
Your family can adapt
They have been through so much worse
Then their daughter saying they aren't a girl or a boy

Be present in the change, Ollie
What has happened is in the rearview mirror
What will happen is 50 miles ahead, exit on the right

Your journey is your own
Other maps do not have to fit you
Like an expensive winter glove

Keep your eyes peeled for danger
Help others, Ollie
But do not do it
At the risk of hurting your car

You're them already, Ollie
I can see it in your eyes
Reflecting a bright future
Keep going, Ollie

No matter what your brain whispers, Ollie
You can be the king of many
Made up to the gods, swaying to Mingus.

# THE OTHER OLLIE

Someone steps onto the
Precipice
Somewhere between girl &
Something we dare not
Mention
A dead name tag is pinned to their lapel
They look about, trying to find
Little glimpses of something
Their professor's scars forefront
They read on how you can make something out
Of previous parts
Worries about pets and snuggles
Transfemme & transmasc
Forget crying at the
Funeral where the professor stood watch
A simulacra of Heaven,
But instead of sin, something
Different
A little harsh, a little butch
Ollie, don't fall into those rabbit holes
Of brands from some country
They'll never give recompense to
Ollie, find a few people
To sprinkle lore onto like breadcrumbs
Ollie, please have an
Abundance of those scraped-up men

Like you
Understand this is
The place for wastes
Artificial growth for something not green
Your good friend
A friend of five years and counting
will ask whenever you call
"Do you want to transfer?"
& you will say no, you
love it
Their ghosts crowd you, do you hear it?
They are those who died in wars unheard of
In the rough beast's trek to Bethlehem
On streets and in buildings now bulldozed with "artisanal" coffee
You will not know these until you meet the professor
With the scar
(he will say he doesn't get paid enough & you know that's true)
you will see them in every in between you
Meet, someone from this world but fallen: Satan, but make it trans
maybe you'll call them angels
Some of them you'll also call friends
They know their task
But for now, you must step off & grab your meal
some underpaid schmuck
made from a glitched computer
You will hold it, manna

from above
"where are you from?"
Everywhere.
in fact, home is in your walls.

## PART THREE:

## A ELDRITCH HORROR IN COLONIALIST GUISE

# AND THE CHILDREN PLAYED: 1 YR AFTER

and the children played, forbidden from touching for fear
of being unwitting plague rats for those
who could not
Get jabbed
With the scientific triumph of our fractured age

And the teens tiktokked
Tenuous, holding onto phones like loved ones
Hands in sleep gorilla gripping
Alt kids, hotties, so-called main characters

And the "essential" workers continued doing their vital work
Stocking shelves, scanning shit, boxing shit, et cetera
Scream'd at by customers, karens, and supervisors alike,
Each presenting their own challenge

And the parents feared
The slightest throat clear
 & Those who whipped their noses: proverbial penises out
In wegmans
Wondering if their child or their neighbor was up next
For the intubation we were told to shelter for two weeks against

 It seems to have lasted a lifetime.

# YOU SAY YOU WANT A REVOLUTION: A POEM AND AN EXPLICATION

I attend the group I've been told will get us free
Bring an end to all that extinguishes our fires
but all you do is sit in a circle
Discuss the names of those we have learned
Pass the whitest torch I've ever seen in my life
gaslight, gatekeep, pseudo-boss
The same old hymns and
No gods, no masters, sure
No war but class war, yes
But what happens when you drop the torch?
Will you start burning us then?

An Explication

I wanted to have the perspective of a marginalized person attending a leftist space, in particular, a local organization allegedly dedicated to "collective liberation." Leftist organizations are critiqued for a lack of diversity, especially in their membership, and I wanted this to reflect that. They are also critiqued for reading more theory than actually improving the lives of those that their theorists discuss, and, in fact, whitewashing and white-knighting those dear to them (coughs in many white leftist men on the Twitter). I'm sure people relate to this, and I hope you feel inspired to change this paradigm.

# BRuTaL: A ERASURE PROEM OF BASTARD OUT OF CAROLINA BY DOROTHY ALLISON

He talked    i could not understand him
I pulled my blanket around the sprinkling of stars   song playing low on the radio the night stars
 I hugged my blanket held
 still
He was shifting me on his thighs   looked into his eyes he smiled first time pushed my skirt to the sideslidhislefthandbetweenmylegsupagainstmy panties begantorockme betweenhisstomachandhiswrist
It made me afraidhisbighandbetweenmylegs hiseyesglitterinthedimlight

Hestartedtalkingagain mama was going to be all right wewereallgoingtobesohappy happy hand hard I
 tooafraidtocry shake wiggle
Kept sayingit'sgonnabeallright
Kept rocking me staring straightahead I
Could see his reflection in the windshield    everything brightand cold                     I
Knew what it was under his hand       a mystery scary and hard sweat running down  smelled strong and nasty he grunted   hewashurtingme!                  i
  Sobbed once he let go of me I held still     I
Could smell something strange bitter on his fingers   ipulledaway made him laughhekeptlaughing   he lifted me slightly  the

Light was grey and pearly     my insides   shake with fear

                                        I was too afraid to open them again   didn't know


Woke up in  bright gray light of full morning  car still and cold.

# CLASS POEM

I'm in one of those writing phases
where ideas zing, a frisbee or boomerang whizzing toward me
And I have to catch it
I am its accomplice, a amanuensis
To deeper and more recherche subjects
I'm not here to analyze some poets who may turn over
In their grave at our shocking suggestions
I'm here to make you laugh and cry
I am a fool in that way, not the kind who's been
Hapless at love, or who entertains the ruler to bite back against
The vitriol spewing his way
The ideas come while I sleep, work, and most importantly
When the professor drones in that lecture tone that makes
you check the clock every 20 seconds to see if it's moving or
stock still, like yourself out of an ancient politeness
I want to fight poetry
Fuck leaving a work that changes everything
I just want a good, old-fashioned fight with some of the people we venerate
And by fight, I mean write a big long poem
That secures my immortality more than
The sand we write their names into
The tide of history washes them away.

# ALL THE WRITERS

You think you can find us at coffee shops
Sipping some 5 dollar concoction
Pausing at self-defined
Times to get the most
Eyeballs on your work

You think you can gaze into
Our abysses at readings
Regardless of how short or long our poems
Are
You just want to pull an Ursula and steal our voice

this poem goes out to those in the glittering world of the literati
They float in circles like a dead fish
This poem goes out to those working two jobs just to make rent
Always tired but holding out hope their manuscript gets accepted
This poem goes out to those bored in infinite Zoom meetings
Putting down a half-formed sonnet to fill the void where notes of summation should be
And then finding a mystic key in the midst of printed words
This poem goes out to the poet's family
Confused but well-meaning allies to the poet's chaos
This poem goes out to the ones I love
Like the rem song, always there
To keep me sane amidst the end of the world as we know it.

# HOW LUCKY WE ARE

how lucky we are to be alive here
in spite of the invisible enemy
we still exist
we hate those who want to divide us
and those without a fabric
I found good British jazz
the kind that makes you imagine a crowd moshing to a tuba
and also found myself
a NB ND queer leftist Jew
Ur local snowflake could never

---

I see old classmates on the trail
picnicking wanting to be the main character
don't they know they die at the end?
Or get so traumatized people see them in a therapist?

---

shit's wild, ya know
All the dogs running round the park reenacting their feral roots
all the headlines pointing to a post-apocalyptic showdown
btwn red and blue
I grow red from the blue rays the sun
Blesses me with
I pose like a child
Newly found cringe
I listen
This one's for you, the boys on the radio, speaking in chaotic
Language
The type that leads to latent anarchism
Everything I do is a love letter to you.

OLLIE SHANE

# YOU HAVE A POWER INSIDE YOU

I've been reading books on how to be right,
that harp-like birdsong platitudes to write
what you know,
and never to listen
to that voice in your head saying "you're fucked"
I write to reach a part deep inside,
that if I believed in reincarnation,
I would be the soul that existed
in every poet, always
the part that pulls on ideas
like a dogsled abandoned
when the handler sways from exhaustion
on the reins,
that guides the hands
like a seance channeling the spirits—
that part that cracks out the words
that wait on the power within,
if you do it my way.

# MY FATHER SAID

*After F. Scott Fitzgerald's The Great Gatsby*

That one must be non-judgemental

I must rebuke
that one must judge

religion says
judge lest ye not be judged

my father said
be impartial

they are dead
I am alive

I am still here
their ashes dissolved

into heaven
along with the others
you can judge my hypocrisies
I did

and look what happened


do you want me to tell you again?

# MY MOTHER SAID

*After F. Scott Fitzgerald's The Great Gatsby*

"You must marry well"

Well, I took her advice
married well in

I found out three years later the green light had withered
away, worn by mismanagement when I returned

after another phone call at the dinner table

How rude!

no one in France understands the structure of propriety
must be because of those [            ](tom taught it to me.)
he sure loves to read
he's very smart
and even though we've had our differences,
I'm sure he
Loves me.

# WE END IN DARKNESS

the crow hawks its alarum
hopefully, I won't come to harm
      here
              in this minuscule town
                  here
                  farming is horrible, but usury strong
I thought this place would be better when I imagined it
            in my fetters in the dirty decadent city
I'd be at one with nature
            like Thoreau
but that's all in a manger, far away
      just like the divine soul
          he never accounted for the follies of humans (I
never knew how to build; I got pneumonia)
as I lay here coughing up my lifeblood
    snow seeps through the cloth
              people are ensconced in their homes
(but they're praying for my doom I know about their part in society hate the outsiders trying to change their wretched lives)
 I remember that crow, and hock up my last breath
                  for crows are the messengers of
doom—

OLLIE SHANE

# ARS POETICA

Every time I log on the bird app
Some poet's making a manifesto

to god, or some other empowered being
advocating another weed strain of political

Action. I found my craft in the margins
in some exalted place between heaven

and hell. there, I went through phases
that would make an emo kid blush.

first, Ginsberg taught me how to tease from grey matter
what he called the muck of the mind

I did it with the finesse
Of someone dissecting a frog

he and I were a love that stretched through the bonds of eternity
sometimes he spoke in bardic chants

That I breathless transcribed
Thus was my poesy for a good while

then I felt 6,000 years rush in front of me
a wave of feeling that if god was on my side

he'd say, all is not lost, Ollie
but he stayed silent when I had my visions

of blake coming to my bed
where I lay, covered in palm fronds and crude simulacra of spaceships

Then I grew hot
and flung them off, I did not know

Where they landed
nor did I want to

Go away, Ginsberg! I shrieked
His muck

Had choked me
I had to leave it behind

So yeah, a few hours
passed like waiting for a delivery driver

I had no one to follow
I will shorten it to this: It felt lonely

Then blake came around
he, enlightened but so

unlike him
he chanted but his told of places

Choked with vowels
fantasmagoric names

Like Golgonooza or

Urthona

names that felt like
A horde surrounding

Me. names that comforted me
like the kaddish does a mourner

he told me each name has a meaning in his prophecies
which he recited, in a trance over that long day

he told me how he was surrounded by los
How I said Milton he said—who? I asked him, he, tears in

his eyes, said the wielder of loss, he showed me
His left foot, there was a clear lump—

He grew taller, I could hear the clink
of a hammer building something from a fiery forge

From somewhere
or maybe it was a car backfiring

I could not tell you how strange it was
to listen to his strange tale

and I believe it rattles in me to this day
Every time I sit at my computer

pecking out my phrases in purplish prose
I remember

a moment when I thought while he told his tale
did I take my medication?

and furiously, I begin
My version of his tale.

# WE SEE WHAT WE WANT TO BELIEVE

papers inked with numbers
fall

in the rubble
of the colonized city

inked with numbers rendered meaningless
thought it could save

the world

dominos fall
and the think tanks make no analysis

no lights in the tunnel
must sense through breathing
self or VC

in the end, body count broke the minds and bodies of so many killing pilgrims in Paradise for what?

for international honor that faded as rapidly as the tides?
I still wake up and think "they are the trees."

# FREAK FLAG

I
limp wristed
like linguini
carrying iced coffee
like a baby

when you see them, the bass and speakers
They
Pulse, their own queer beat
In the club where my kin meet

trade reads, trades
Like baseball cards
With their own rewards in the collection

I
Shy away from displays of affection
The bass and speakers
Make me scream: remnants of the ward
Implanted in my subconscious

I
Prefer my artist's queer
Those deemed too faggy
For the mainstream

Too rare to live free
From the gears of society

Too weird to exist
w/out the cishet gaze
On their ars poetica

I
Love to watch them
Dip, rant, and rave

Freaks in solidarity
With comrades like us
Who needs cishets?

# WHEN AUTOCORRECT CORRECTS "BRING" TO "BEING" REGARDING BOOKS

books are the place in which my heart resides
maybe the other way around?
wake up/sleep/in gorgeous covers
Once, during an anxiety attack,Ii slept with a book on my left
its hardness I woke up on in the morning

I was drawn to books
they loved me
The feeling was mutual

If I could choose where I lived, it would be on top of a bookstore
So I could peruse the literature at my leisure—a Victorian fantasy

If someone tells me they love books, they quickly become my entire world
My sounding board for ranting about the complexity of loving something so (in)finite

If I was reincarnated, I would be inside of Allen Ginsberg
as he stopped jerking off when a perceived mentor spirit spoke
as he wrote the poems that defined him
as he howled obscenities at a whitewashed government

If I could dream freely, it would be as a god
curled up in the stuffy bookshelves of city lights.

OLLIE SHANE

# THE THING ABOUT OLLIE

Limp wristed
O Hallelujah, that's me

Always ready with a quip about what they've been through
O Hallelujah, that's me

wearing shitkickers like a soldier in war
O Hallelujah, that's me

So young before growing—rapidly—old
O Hallelujah, that's me

College student—though not this semester
O Hallelujah, that's me

eldritch horror in colonialist guise
O Hallelujah, that's me

Lover of those who could not love themselves
O Hallelujah, that's

Me.

# ODE TO SHITKICKERS

the only doc I trust
Lay on my feet like a lapdog
Or a trusted lover
Every day,
I tromp about
Attending my anxiety
Like a soldier at war
Baggy, black camo pants, army-green jacket
Looking like an American soldier
the American imaginary

Oh, shitkickers
Known for your beatings
To those unworthy
Of your wasted love
Lay your booted foot
On my lily-white neck
Listen to my gasps of pleasure and pain
As you show me who's the one
In charge.

# ODE TO MY SPORTS BRA

You
Are a geometric thing of beauty
Help shape the balloon'd breasts
into something resembling
The men I brush by in school

their stares
Marking me the antagonist
In a horror film
The one to be an object

To be exterminated
A bug to be quashed
A reason for a keg party
The kind where you stumble around
Drunk as a [          ]

do you know that the warm feeling you get from imbibing alcohol
Is it a lie?
I say to anyone who so much as
Gazes in my direction
You do not turn warm
As a hearth fire
I continue


you freeze like the little matchgirl

The [ ] in the corner notices my male guise
and says
Nice binding

I blush
I want to kiss them
Till their lips turn a fiery red from
My ministrations.

# I AM AUTISM

Hello [      ]
Praise be
when those who you called friends said
look at that [   ]
What a [     ]
Because your mind
Blanked when theirs didn't
Never could ride a skateboard
But could recite all
The poets from the 19th century
At the drop of a hat


Then you had
Those urges
To walk, stim, laugh
Others walked around you, saw your stimming
And laughed
For years, you were the ridicule
Others used to make you feel
Insignificant
Used you to get away from
Their stigmata
So they put their bloody wounds on
You to heal them
Always taken, never the taker


And you wanted to bash your head
Make it raw and bloody

So all could see
The pain that went inside you for days and days
Trying to be perfect, trying to do SOMETHING
Anything,
To strip off the harlequin costume
They forced you into
You had to find me

I did not destroy you
They did
But you can't kill them, I don't advocate that
Rather
I ask you
To
Put on an oxygen mask
Then the harlequin will fall

And you will be left
in its
ashes.

# NOT IN THE MIDDLE OF A...

When we say...

Pandemonium (we must be accustomed to crouching at the margins of the world)

Panacotta (sweet to be away, but only for a while--right?)

Panera bread (where I got my order of home tasting soup, remembering my library meals equals a new place)
Panda Express (the grains of fried rice used to melt, now I bloat from its richness)
panderer (to those who want eternal chaos)
Panoramic (time stretches out to the bounds)


We actually mean
Pandemic
But we've said it for so long
that we have to come up with other ways of speaking
The unspeakable.

# A COUNTING

you died, Ma, so someone had to do it
Sort through what to take to goodwill
& what to keep, to show to my siblings and grandchildren
Shook up by their beloved Mother and Meemaw six feet under
Sure, there was comfort in your blankets, your books on such inanities
As the hallmark channel and the nature of G-d
We fed the dog the food you gave him before we took him to the vet
Although you and Dad loved Sparky, it's harder to pay bills with a pet
& their various, unknowable illnesses to look after
We divvied up your possessions, ma
By who had the best stories to tell
Brother Pat took the painting by some local fop
And sister cat took the deformed pot from some enrichment attempt
I lunged for the ashtray, counting the rings of cigarette burns you'd put into me
When I did nothing but be a kid.

# TWOFACE

> "I was the same as you: less a person and more a hole cut away from everything"—Everything Under by Daisy Johnson

at first, you were a dog sniffing my crotch
then you were an unknowable terror

Unrecognizable
to my all-knowing eyes

glean'd from the pile of books
On my drawer

You crept ever closer
To my mouth

I wriggling
a fish caught on a line

Your maw opened
And I saw

The cosmos
Reflected as pins in your jaws

Unknowable amounts of light
Flooded in me

I shudder when I think
of your power over me

I screamed
reverberated in my ass and spine

& then I woke.

# A ELDRITCH HORROR IN COLONIALIST GUISE, OR, WHAT IF KURTZ AND MARLOWE WERE GAY

I. the sotadic zone

Forever in your thrall,
I followed
You up the tumescent river
Reminiscent of your penis
In this, the most essential
Of holes
I penetrated in that long African night
the one that I knew from my time as a sailor
gay with men like me
covered in tattoos
Little gods I could warp
For my own benefit
The sky looks like heaven tonight
I can almost imagine Milton's seraphim
Descending to serenade us
With their weird music
In rhymes, no mortal could ape

until I came to this shithole country
Somewhere khaki doesn't stay
Somewhere you went feral
Childs posed 2 our common root
Married the most hated creature
Woman
In all her devious glory

so I had to find and kill you.


ii. if i can't touch you/a knife or gun will do


so I had to find and kill you
Fuckers got pissed that you went off the grid

But honestly, who would blame you? I said
After our first time when you

Made your mouth a pipeline
To the most-prized treasure

Your cock

A beauty to behold

I wonder if your wife can give you what you want

I could


We could have been BELOVED

you in ur khaki uniform
the sexiest soldier of my wettest of dreams

I your rock
Keeping you pinned
To solid ground

but no, you had to fuck it up.


iii. became the sailor boy/became the company man/but i can't become you

but no, you had to fuck it up.

they
told me to kill you

I agreed and here I am

Cruising down the river
its stolid crew
Terrified of your name
Cowers as they go about their essential tasks

whispers your name in awe

you are a god

you stride, an overgrown child

your toys: machines from cast-off empires

that abandoned, too bogged down

in local milieu

your exploits whisper'd

to lovers in the throes

of passion sent down

from those on high
—

we used to be like that

do you remember?

that night, you whispered to me

Something about injecting kids with polio or some other deadly pathogen

I didn't care, I needed

that dick buried
in me

Yet the only burial that happened
Was that of your trauma from

Becoming the death squad of Vietnamese children

in some shitty castaway clothing of a
town

you became the man

I know and love

I had to kill that which I love

I wasn't given the choice

that you did
—

did you care about me?

when we made love, did you scream my name like a prayer to some far-flung god?

would you bleed for me?

I have my answer
in front of me

I made you my stuffed pig-boy

Ev'ry orifice mine to conquer

My troy
To pillage.

# ACKNOWLEDGEMENTS

I would like to thank Nimbus and their work on creating a kind and inclusive writer community at Bryn Mawr College. Without their work, I would be just another voice, screaming into a seemingly infinite void. Without Nimbus, I never would have met Ariya Bandy, who is another amazing poet. If you like my works, I'd recommend her book Painted Winds, which iYou are doing amazing things in the world of poetry and I'm proud to be writing in

Speaking of magazines, I would like to thank Dipity Literary Magazine, the Amazine, Fizz, and Written in the Stars Magazine for featuring my poems before I put them into this full length . It meant a lot to this beginning writer to get acceptances for my poetry and the chance to put my works out there.

I would also like to thank the Wellington Square Bookshop poetry writing group for their enthusiasm and encouragement for my work. This book would not exist without your space to let me share my works and get feedback from others.

To the Wild Ink publishing family, including, but not limited to Johnny Francis Wolf, Bruce Buchanan (author and Braves fan, don't worry, he's nice about it), Abigail Taylor, and Rebecca Minelga. You took one of the younger poets/authors in the group and embraced me as one of your own. I appreciate the Slack conversations and Google Meet hangouts.

To my friends, both named and unnamed here: Deema, Julia, Brinkley and the entire Gritty Family, Jared, Maddy Rachel, thank you for being there with me.

And finally, I would like to thank my family, especially my mom, dad, Nonny, sister, Grandma, Grandpa, John Tassoni (a second cousin of mine who writes poetry and teaches English) and many more. Your support has helped me so much, from taking me to my monthly poetry groups to reading my poems to saying how proud you are of my work. It means a lot.

Ollie Shane is a poet, recent graduate from Bryn Mawr College, prospective librarian, and the number one tote bag carrier and coffee sipper in the Tri-State Area (Delaware and Pennsylvania). He is Autistic and their special interest revolves around literature (currently on 20th century literature (such as W. Somerset Maugham, who they've doing their thesis on) in conjunction with contemporary poets such as Danez Smith, sam sax, Franny Choi, Terrance Hayes, Mary Alice Daniel and others). Also, he is constantly looking for more poetry and prose recommendations.

On a writerly note, they are the author of the chapbook I Do It So It Feels Like Hell (Bottlecap Press, 2022), and their work has been published in Thirty West's magazine AfterImages, Poetry As Promised, Palindrome Journal, and elsewhere. They also have a newsletter on Substack called Not Another Newsletter. To see more of their work, check him out on Instagram @aolshane and Chill Subs under olshane17.

www.ingramcontent.com/pod-product-compliance
Lightning Source LLC
Chambersburg PA
CBHW021943140125
20374CB00004B/142